Published by Concordia Publishing House
3558 S. Jefferson Avenue, St. Louis, MO 63118-3968
1-800-325-3040 • www.cph.org
Illustrations copyright © 2006 by David Erickson

1 2 3 4 5 6 7 8 9 10   15 14 13 12 11 10 09 08 07 06

He Is Risen, Indeed!

Paintings by David Erickson

TEXT FROM THE HOLY BIBLE, ENGLISH STANDARD VERSION

CONCORDIA PUBLISHING HOUSE · SAINT LOUIS

It was now about the sixth hour, and there was darkness over the whole land until the ninth hour, while the sun's light failed. And the curtain of the temple was torn in two. Then Jesus, calling out with a loud voice, said, " *Father, into Your hands I commit My spirit!*" And having said this He breathed His last. Now when the centurion saw what had taken place, he praised God, saying, "Certainly this man was innocent!" And all the crowds that had assembled for this spectacle, when they saw what had taken place, returned home beating their breasts. And all His acquaintances and the women who had followed Him from Galilee stood at a distance watching these things.

Luke 23:44–49

When it was evening, there came a rich man from Arimathea, named Joseph, who also was a disciple of Jesus. He went to Pilate and asked for the body of Jesus. Then Pilate ordered it to be given to him. …

Joseph took the body and wrapped it in a clean linen shroud and laid it in his own new tomb, which he had cut in the rock.

And he rolled a great stone to the entrance of the tomb and went away. Mary Magdalene and the other Mary were there, sitting opposite the tomb.

Matthew 27:57–61

When the Sabbath was past, Mary Magdalene and Mary the mother of James and Salome bought spices, so that they might go and anoint Him.

And very early on the first day of the week, when the sun had risen, they went to the tomb.

And they were saying to one another, "Who will roll away the stone for us from the entrance of the tomb?"

Mark 16:1–3

And behold, there was a great earthquake, for an angel of the Lord descended from heaven and came and rolled back the stone and sat on it. His appearance was like lightning, and his clothing white as snow. *And for fear of him the guards trembled and became like dead men.*

Matthew 28:2–4

While they were perplexed about this, behold, two men stood by them in dazzling apparel. And as they were frightened and bowed their faces to the ground, the men said to them, "Why do you seek the living among the dead?

He is not here, but has risen.

Remember how He told you, while He was still in Galilee, that the Son of Man must be delivered into the hands of sinful men and be crucified and on the third day rise."

Luke 24:4–7

"But go, tell His disciples
and Peter that
He is going before you
to Galilee.

There you will see Him, just as
He told you." And they went
out and fled from the tomb,
for trembling and astonishment
had seized them, and they said
nothing to anyone, for they
were afraid.

Mark 16:7–8

And they remembered His words,

*and returning from the
tomb they told all these
things to the eleven
and to all the rest.*

Now it was Mary Magdalene
and Joanna and Mary the mother
of James and the other women with
them who told these things to the
apostles, but these words seemed
to them an idle tale, and they
did not believe them.

Luke 24:8–11

So Peter went out with the other disciple, and they were going toward the tomb. Both of them were running together, but the other disciple outran Peter and reached the tomb first. And stooping to look in, he saw the linen cloths lying there, but he did not go in. Then Simon Peter came, following him, and went into the tomb. He saw the linen cloths lying there, and the face cloth, which had been on Jesus' head, not lying with the linen cloths but folded up in a place by itself. Then the other disciple, who had reached the tomb first, also went in, *and he saw and believed;* for as yet they did not understand the Scripture, that He must rise from the dead. Then the disciples went back to their homes.

John 20:3–10

Mary stood weeping outside the tomb. … She turned around and saw Jesus standing, but she did not know that it was Jesus. … Supposing Him to be the gardener, she said to Him, "Sir, if you have carried Him away, tell me where you have laid Him, and I will take Him away." Jesus said to her, *"Mary."* She turned and said to Him in Aramaic, *"Rabboni!"* (which means Teacher). Jesus said to her, "Do not cling to Me, for I have not yet ascended to the Father; but go to My brothers and say to them, 'I am ascending to My Father and your Father, to My God and your God.'" Mary Magdalene went and announced to the disciples, *"I have seen the Lord"* —and that He had said these things to her.

John 20:11–18

After these things He appeared
in another form to two of them, as
they were walking into the country.
*And they went back
and told the rest, but
they did not believe them.*

Mark 16:12–13

On the evening of that day, the first day of the week, the doors being locked where the disciples were for fear of the Jews, Jesus came and stood among them and said to them, "Peace be with you." When He had said this, He showed them His hands and His side. Then the disciples were glad when they saw the Lord. Jesus said to them again, *"Peace be with you. As the Father has sent Me, even so I am sending you."*

And when He had said this, He breathed on them and said to them, "Receive the Holy Spirit. If you forgive the sins of anyone, they are forgiven; if you withhold forgiveness from anyone, it is withheld."

John 20:19–23

Now Jesus did many other signs in the presence
of the disciples, which are not written in this book;
but these are written so that you may believe
that Jesus is the Christ, the Son of God, and that
by believing you may have life in His name.

John 20:30–31